Ikebana
Is Better Than
Therapy!

SUSUMU UYEDA

Designed and Illustrated by
Lianne U. Liang

厚子 ATSUKO
PUBLISHING

• Ikebana Is Better Than Therapy! •

SUSUMU UYEDA

Design and Illustration:
Lianne U. Liang,
Liang Publication & Production Services

厚子
ATSUKO PUBLISHING
8116 Arlington Boulevard, Suite 164
Falls Church, Virginia 22042
www.atsukopublish.com

Copyright© 2004 by Susumu Uyeda
All rights reserved. Printed in the United States of America.
No part of this book may be used or reproduced in any manner whatsoever
without written permission except in the case of brief quotations
embodied in critical articles and reviews.
For information, address Atsuko Publishing.

FIRST EDITION

Ikebana Is Better Than Therapy™ 2004

ISBN 0-9665467-1-7
Library of Congress Control Number 2003097109

If you would like to share any thoughts about this book or
are interested in other books and products by Atsuko Publishing,
please write to our address above.

In 1998, my daughter, Roxanne A. Uyeda, published a book titled, "Shopping Is Better Than Therapy." Since I was heavily into ikebana, I thought it might be fun to write a companion book, "Ikebana Is Better Than Therapy"; this is the result.

This book contains rather whimsical and fun thoughts with a sprinkling of food for thought that many ikebana people probably have experienced or encountered. Ikebana, as most of you know, is the art of Japanese flower arranging. Its documented history goes back almost 600 years.

It embodies Japanese love for nature and their sense of beauty. It has become popular and practiced worldwide and now knows no national or cultural boundaries. At the same time, it has evolved with contemporary changes in society, thinking, living and working environments. It is generally accepted that it has a calming effect on the practitioners. If you are a nonbeliever, you may wish to try ikebana and prove to yourself that indeed "Ikebana Is Better Than Therapy."

Happy and enjoyable reading to all of you, and may this book allow you to forget whatever is troubling you even for a short moment.

....

Hearty words of appreciation go to my three daughters:
Lianne U. Liang (Liang Publication & Production Services),
who provided the design and illustrations for this book;
Roxanne A. Uyeda, who gave me the idea for this book and who shared her experience with me sparing me from spinning my wheels; and Vivianne C. Uyeda, whose dry sense of humor is highly infectious and set the tone of this book.

Special thanks goes to my wife, Kiyoko, who is an accomplished and well-known ikebana teacher of Ikenobo, who unknowingly and unwittingly gave me many of the ideas contained in this book and who encouraged me to forge ahead. Who can forget our grandchildren, Jennifer and Justin, who have served as the fountain of youth providing constant streams of physical and mental challenges? Also, the author expresses his gratitude to all his ikebana friends and teachers who gave him many of the ideas and thoughts in this book and for their support and encouragement.

....

DISCLAIMER: *The contents of this book are meant to be taken lightly and are in no way intended to offend anyone, especially those who provide or seek professional psychological or psychiatric services.*

1

Wonderful,
> wonderful things ensue
when we allow
the beauty of the flowers
> to reside in our hearts.

2

Psychiatrists, beware!

Ikebana is

challenging

> your profession.

3

Her routine used to be…

    home, doctor's office,

home, doctor's office,

    home…

Now, it's home, ikebana class,

    home, ikebana class,

    home…

Hiking trails turn into

wonderful ikebana classrooms:

    Oh, there is the perfect branch!

  If I combine that one,

      this one, and this one,

  I'd have the ideal

      ikebana arrangement.

Oh, there's another

    perfect one, and another,

    and another…

She tried every which way
to conceive, but to no avail.
　　Now that she has been taking
　　ikebana lessons,
　she and her husband are
　　　the proud parents of three
rambunctious, but
　　　　adorable, toddlers.

6

*T*ry smiling at the flowers and they will smile back at you.

If shopping is better

than therapy,

and if ikebana is better

than therapy,

which do I choose?

(Shopping can cost you!)

That has to wait

for another time…

I'm off to

ikebana class now.

The flowers continue to smile, even though the teacher severely criticizes your arrangement. They, too, can empathize, you know.

10

*M*ake a statement…
flower arrangements
for peace, harmony, and
goodwill among all people.

Car pools to

    ikebana classes

bloom into beautiful

    and lasting friendships.

Yellowing flag iris leaves, some with browning tips. We arrange them to honor and appreciate their hard work for having produced magnificent arrays of flowers during the summer months.

Ikebana:

> For me, an infinite source of joy and serenity.
>
> For the cat, just another source of drinking water.

Driving two

to three hours for an

ikebana workshop

must be motivated by

more than a sheer

desire to learn more

about ikebana…

therapy, maybe?

Driving two

to three hours to

teach ikebana must

be motivated by more

than a sheer desire to

teach and promote it…

therapy, maybe?

16

In pursuing ikebana, don't become a mechanic, become an artist.

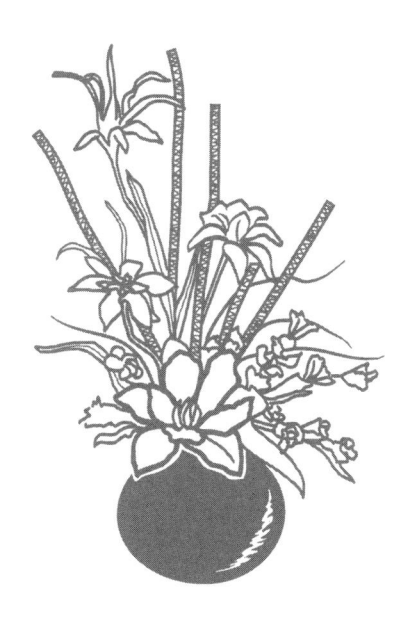

Psychiatrists' chairs are soft;

ikebana lessons are hard.

Well, don't we need

hard challenges?

Repressing the urge

    to rearrange her

birthday gift of

    a dozen roses

in ikebana-style,

I politely

compliment them.

19

When you're bending a branch with force, the trick is to stop before it snaps.

Through happiness or adversity, flowers never cease to smile.

When I do ikebana,

I never look at the clock.

Moreover, more often

than not, I forget

my coffee and snacks.

22

Ikebana, in its own right, is therapy!

Hey wait a minute!

If ikebana is better

    than therapy, and

    if ikebana is therapy

    in and of itself,

how can it be

    better than itself?

When one becomes hooked on ikebana, it becomes a life-long learning process. I hope I live that long!

25

Ikebana is a great medicine for stress…and how!!!

No matter how

        hard one tries,

a beautiful arrangement

        cannot be preserved…

except in memories.

Political affiliations, ethnic backgrounds and religious beliefs make no difference in ikebana classes.

Ikebana is better

   than therapy…

try it twice a week

   for five weeks and,

then, come see me, again.

Ikebana husbands should be
saluted for their support,
help, patience and
understanding without which
ikebana expert "wannabes"
cannot go forward so gallantly.

The world's greatest worry-buster is ikebana, ikebana, and more ikebana.

The beauty of ikebana

is in the eyes of the observers…

and especially in the

eyes of the arrangers.

When we begin to understand and appreciate ikebana, we begin to see inside the hearts of the arrangers.

Did you know that skunk cabbages are protected as national treasures in certain parts of Japan? The flowers resemble the image of Buddha and are revered.

Ikebana must

>be easy because

it uses only

>a few stems.

If you agree,

>think again.

When you bring in

flowers from the garden,

it is your duty

to make them all

the more beautiful

in your arrangement.

Students of ikebana can be

divided into two groups.

In one group are those who are

seeking instant diversion

and relaxation.

In the other are those who want

to become expert arrangers

as quickly as possible.

The best and lasting students are

somewhere in between.

When you're concentrating on

where to bend this branch

and where to place that flower,

the world's troubles seem

so distant and obscure.

We should have a national holiday to recognize and appreciate the joy and enjoyment that flowers give us during the year.

They are a perfect couple.

He is an "ikebana widower,"
and she is a "golf widow."

When he is going for a
hole in one, she is creating
the perfect arrangement.

Every once in a while,

    one hears a story about

a beginner bringing poison ivy

    to an ikebana class.

Yes, ikebana does require

    knowledge about plants.

But to acquire that knowledge,

    one does not have to

suffer through a rough,

    and sometimes, itchy path.

Hey, it is better

to get hooked

on ikebana than

on drugs or alcohol.

Ikebana is for the birds?

Then, it must be for

the peace-loving doves.

She (the wife) thinks

she is the world's

greatest ikebana artist.

He (the husband) thinks

he is a greater critic.

Happiness is when the flowers used in an ikebana class two weeks ago are still fresh and alive.

It is called

   "volunteer pruning"

when one quietly

   acquires a few branches

from the city park.

Holidays, birthdays, and other special occasions are all opportunities to show off ikebana skills.

47

*I*nstant serenity…

through ikebana.

Fact or fiction?

The genesis of ikebana

was a lotus leaf used

as a lid on a water jug

in ancient China.

Ikebana husbands are precious.
They drive you to ikebana
meetings, help with loading and
unloading ikebana paraphernalia,
take you out when you're famished
after ikebana activities,
provide moral support and,
oh yes, climb trees to get you
the perfect branches you want.

Really?

In New York City?

In a taxicab?

A miniature ikebana

greeting customers?

It's the truth,

so help me God!

*H*appiness is when

you find an ikebana container

you always wanted

at a yard sale.

(…and a steal at that!)

Sniffling and sneezing,

ikebana enthusiasts

with allergies are

hardly deterred.

Are they crazy or what?

a dish of hard candies

at an ikebana class…

tempting, but

more importantly,

a study in

color coordination

and color contrast.

My blood pressure?

I don't know.

I don't check it, anymore…

not since I started

ikebana classes.

Smile, when you overcome the temptation to "adopt" the ideal branch from your neighbor's yard.

When I started ikebana,

I didn't know what I was doing.

Ten years later,

I still don't know what I am doing.

But, I'm having a barrel of fun.

Golfers and ikebana students:

Similarities:

When all goes well,

they feel great and relaxed.

If not, they feel frustrated.

Dissimilarities:

When golfers miss a putt,

they blurt out unprintable words.

When ikebana students

accidentally break

a branch,

they grin and bear it.

In lieu of peace talks,

why not ikebana sessions?

In lieu of light jail sentences,

why not mandatory

ikebana lessons?

Years ago, there used to be an advertising slogan that said,

"I'd walk a mile for a …"

Today, our slogan is,

"We'd drive hundreds of miles for a good ikebana lesson."

Together, the flowers

are begging

    the question,

"Why can't humans

    live in peace?"

Tropical flowers and indigenous materials, when combined, add spice to ikebana.

Freedom has its price –

a poignant message

    from a lone stem of a

flower put in a glass

    at the voting place.

Even if only one more person takes up ikebana, the world will be a better place.

God created flowers
to decorate the world.
God created people
to beautify and pacify the world.
Well, when do we start?

Once you enter

    the tranquil world

of ikebana,

    you will never want

to leave it.

If you are against harmony,

peace and goodwill

among all people,

ikebana is not for you.

Soap operas will have to take a backseat.

Ikebana class, here I come!

Explore ikebana.

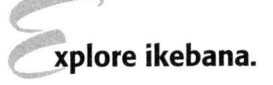

Discover yourself.

Now that the children are gone,

dishes done, laundry in the dryer,

    and house cleaning finished,

she is faced with a major decision…

    does she take a nap or do ikebana?

Her solution:

    ikebana now, nap later.

70

Ikebana, a preview of heaven.

A penny for my thoughts?

Well, here goes.

Did you know that a copper coin

placed in water prolongs

the life of certain cut flowers?

And did you know that a

penny inserted between the

petals of an unopened tulip

will delay its opening?

a toddler, hardly able to walk, points to the ikebana on the table and exclaims, "BA-NA-NA!" "BA-NA-NA!"

Yes, I admit that

    I am "high" on ikebana,

but I really don't need or

    want a detoxification program.

WANTED: More young persons to carry the torch for ikebana!

The cats, I thought,

were quite impressed

with my ikebana…

until one of them took a

swipe at a swaying branch.

In Japan, the master of the house did ikebana. In the United States, the master of the house does ikebana. Translation: In Japan, husbands used to do ikebana. In the United States, wives do ikebana.

Our sorrows and adversities

pale into the background

    when we focus on ikebana.

Ikebana on

> the coffee table…

a great

> conversation piece.

Now, what did

> we get together for?

Ikebana classes are

like sponges…

    they absorb

    your tension, rage,

        worries and fear.

*Happiness is when

you win a blue ribbon

for your ikebana at

a local garden club exhibit.*

WANTED: More males

to partake in ikebana

to bring out the

qualities and perspectives

that only they can.

Invisible things we try

to capture in ikebana:

    the gentle breeze,

the fond memories

    triggered by the flora,

and the joyful feelings

    suddenly brought on

by a single flower.

The world needs

        and deserves

more laughter…

        and ikebana.

When following

doctor's orders,

sneak in a

few ikebana sessions

and your recovery

will be twice as fast.

85

Ikebana...
a magnificent
obsession!

Ikebana was not

        her first love.

But it was,

        for sure, her last.

Bless her soul.

87

Ikebana a day keeps the doctor away.

The precious time

>   one invests

in ikebana

>   could prolong

one's life.

In Japan where

> people experience

the greatest longevity

in the world,

ikebana practitioners

> enjoy even longer lives.

The Headmaster of one of the leading schools urges people to arrange flowers with their feet. Translation: Walk the countryside, hike to the mountaintops, and stroll along the streams to observe the raw character, characteristics, and growth habits of each plant. And reflect those observations and knowledge in your ikebana.

No matter how much the
world changes in politics,
 technologies, social situations
and environments,
 there will always be ikebana
because people will continue
 to need and pursue it as
 a ready source for instant serenity.

We, the ikebana devotees

hereby proclaim,

"Ikebana is better

than therapy!"

"…IKEBANA IS BETTER

THAN THERAPY!"

"…IKEBANA IS BETTER

THAN THERAPY!"